AF575800

BACKYARD SCIENCE

How a Garden Grows

Miranda Kelly

TABLE OF CONTENTS

A Crabtree Seedlings Book

CRABTREE
Publishing Company
www.crabtreebooks.com

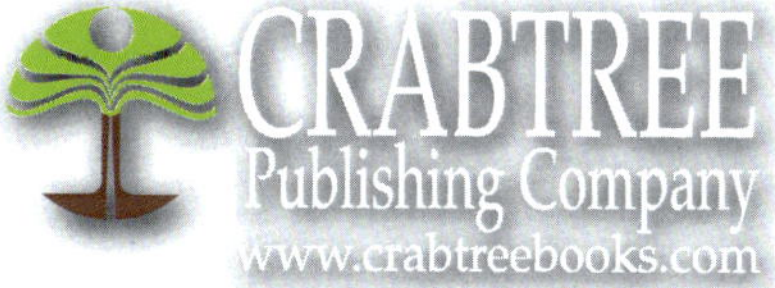

HOW A GARDEN GROWS

People grow food to eat.

We grow food in a **garden.**

We grow **fruits** and **vegetables.**

We plant **seeds** to start a garden.

Sunlight and water make the seeds grow.

We use garden **tools**.

Tools help us do jobs.

Butterfl
diner

With hard work, the **plants** will grow big.

Now we can pick the food from the garden.

It's time to eat.

YUM!

Glossary

fruits (FROOTS): Fruits are parts of plants that we eat. Fruits have seeds.

garden (GAR-duhn): A garden is where plants such as flowers, vegetables, and shrubs are grown.

plants (PLANTS): Plants are living things that usually have a stem, leaves, and sometimes flowers and fruit.

seeds (SEEDZ): Seeds are the parts of a plant from which new plants can grow.

tools (TOOLS): Tools are objects we use to do different jobs. A shovel is a tool we use to dig in a garden.

vegetables (VEJ-tuh-bulz): Vegetables are parts of plants that we eat. Vegetables do not have seeds.

Index

School-to-Home Support for Caregivers and Teachers

This book helps children grow by letting them practice reading. Here are a few guiding questions to help the reader build his or her comprehension skills. Possible answers appear here in red.

Before Reading

- **What do I think this book is about?** I think this book is about how to grow vegetables in a garden. I think this book is about the steps you need to take in order to grow food.
- **What do I want to learn about this topic?** I want to learn more about how deep a seed should be placed in the soil. I want to learn everything about growing vegetables.

During Reading

- **I wonder why...** I wonder why vegetables don't have seeds. I wonder why vegetables are planted in straight rows.
- **What have I learned so far?** I have learned that the first step to growing food is to plant a seed. I have learned that seeds need sunlight and water to grow.

After Reading

- **What details did I learn about this topic?** I have learned that the fruit of a plant contains the seeds. I have learned that vegetables don't have seeds.
- **Read the book again and look for the glossary words.** I see the word *tools* on page 12, and the word *plants* on page 17. The other glossary words are found on pages 22 and 23.

Library and Archives Canada Cataloguing in Publication

CIP available at Library and Archives Canada

Library of Congress Cataloging-in-Publication Data

CIP available at Library of Congress

Crabtree Publishing Company
www.crabtreebooks.com 1–800–387–7650

Written by: Miranda Kelly

Production coordinator and Prepress technician: Tammy McGarr

Print coordinator: Katherine Berti

Print book version produced jointly with Blue Door Education in 2022

Printed in Canada/062022/CPC20220603

PHOTO CREDITS:
Photo credits: Cover photo © bokan76 - i-stockphoto.com. All other images from Shutterstock.com: green box graphic throughout © By Kelvin Degree, page 2-3 © Morinka; page 4 © Irina Fischer, page 5 © lovelyday12; page 6 © Africa Studio, page 7 © allstars; page 8 © Caron Badkin, page 9 © kazoka; page 10-11 © lovelyday12; page 12-13 and title page photo © Abramova Elena; pages 14, 15, 16 © Rawpixel.com, page 17 © Ailisa; page 18-19 © gorillaimages; page 20-21 © Toey Toey

Published in the United States
Crabtree Publishing
347 Fifth Ave.
Suite 1402-145
New York, NY 10016

Published in Canada
Crabtree Publishing
616 Welland Ave.
St. Catharines, Ontario
L2M 5V6